RABBIT EARS TO CABLE

Rabbit Ears to Cable

Journal Of Our Autism Family.

by
Summer Nauss

Dorrance Publishing Co
585 Alpha Drive
Pittsburgh, PA 15238
Visit our website at www.dorrancebookstore.com

ISBN: 979-8-89127-536-2
eISBN: 979-8-89127-034-3

RABBIT EARS TO CABLE

I've been raising autism for 25 years.

When I started this journey with my daughter, there was one word to diagnosis her. Autistic

Now there more types of autism than Baskin Robbins's 31 flavors.

Aspergers, Kanners, Rett Syndrome, Sensory Disorder, 1 level, 2 level, 3 level, audio sensory disorder, autism with others disorders. Those are endless.

When I talk with younger mothers, they are just starting their autism journey.

It all sounds so alien to me.

They seem to brag about having a place in an autism category.

As if there is some prestige to having a category.

Talk to me at three a.m. when they have bitten their finger down to the cartilage. No pain.

When you can't have sex in your home. Their radars pick up on every single sound or mood change in 2.6 seconds. Followed by the world as we know it is ending because of a piece of lint on their pants.

If these things don't line up in the right category, does that mean they don't exist?

I assure you the look on my husband's face after hundreds of attempts for sex tells me screw your categories and levels of autism.

I can't bring myself to have a conversation with the young newbie parents of autistics.

The categories are not important.

Talk to me about your CODE RED plan when wi-fi goes out.

Show me the face you make when someone says, "Your child doesn't look autistic!"

Confess how many glasses of wine does it take for you to prepare for IEP meetings?

In the autism world, there are good and bad days. Days we are just trying to get through it without huddling in a corner, sucking your thumb, asking, "Has anyone seen my baseball?"

My daughter was officially diagnosed at UCD Mindd Institute.

She has participated in many research studies on autism.

Research scientists and doctors from all over the world. Studying Autism.

It was here I learned high functioning; low functioning was not used by them.

Regional centers and schools began using these terms to get state funding for occupational services.

I see law firm commercials claiming this product is linked to autism. If you were pregnant and took this product, call them. You could be entitled to significant compensation.

One night, I was wide-eyed with only the TV glowing in the dark. A law commercial came on.

What the heck. I took Tylenol when I was pregnant. Why not get money over their ignorance?

I know, I know I was tired and angry at the world. I called.

If your autistic child is 18 or older, you do not qualify. Makes no sense to me. This product was taken by pregnant women starting in 1955.

If it is linked to autism, why wouldn't all autistics qualify?

My question still goes unanswered.

I think about the journey I've been on with my autistic daughter. Year after year my questions, worries, challenges change.

I am fast approaching a question that haunts all parents of autistics.

What happens to them when we die?

I'm not talking formalities of healthcare, income or housing.

There is no one on this earth that will get her like I do. Who's going to have the patience like I have?

There's only one answer.

I must never die. I must live forever.

I remember the early days. The thought of me dying was way out in left field.

I remember everything like it was yesterday.

I got texts and calls from family and friends every time an autistic is belting out incredible songs.

A new TV show has an autistic doctor, detective, or college professor.

When I heard a contestant on a televised beauty contest was autistic, I turned off my phone, turned off the lights, and hid.

If there is a special on autism, everyone thinks I should watch, as if it's going to bring some new insight to me.

I felt like I wasn't trying hard enough, not pushing her to be all that she can be.

After one show, they all consider themselves experts on my daughter.

I know they mean well.

My daughter has been in dance. The noise left her on the floor with her fingers in her ears. Everyone dancing around her. Careful not to step on her.

She was happy to lay there. No concept of her disruption.

The most interest she showed was in 4H. My son was in FFA.

As the other kids were learning to ride horses, she would take an old horse named Doc by the reins and walk him around the arena. Lap after lap. Never aware of the riders, trying to get around her.

I've got two boys finding their way in life, staying one step ahead of my boys. With my Aussie daughter in tow, it brings a whole new meaning to living on the edge.

In our world, when my daughter tries a NEW food, that's incredible. When she sleeps, that's astonishing. Her knowledge of anime is mind-blowing.

When she doesn't jump out of her skin after you hug her, well, that's just damn amazing.

This is good enough for me; it's good enough for my daughter and it needs to be good enough for everybody else.

Another year gone. We are no closer to figuring out what causes autism.

It seems the politicians are jumping on board, determining where the money should go. Research, prevention, or cure?

As the politicians battle it out at the state and federal levels, our Aussies are growing up in a world that isn't designed for them. I had bigger battles to fight.

Jan 1st, 2012

United States stopped making iridescent light bulbs. Maybe you all slept through this. It didn't make the headlines.

For autistic parents, this was "Breaking News." Don't change their light bulbs. They're the only bulbs they cannot hear working. Florescent lights hum.

Or so Aussies say. I personally can't hear it.

Autistic parents hit the streets, stores, family and friends in search of these light bulbs.

When I checked the internet, one light bulb was going for 60.00.

As my supply of light bulbs started to dwindle, I wondered how long it would be before I found myself meeting shady characters in alleys, buying light bulbs out of the trunk of cars, from a man named "No Neck."

I wondered what the charge is, for transporting illegal light bulbs from Mexico to the US.

Headline Reads:

Women attempting to smuggle illegal paraphernalia across the US/Mexico Border. Women Arrested.

We are seeing a new doctor.

He came in, sat down, and asked, "So tell me about Pooh?"

"Huh? What? You tell me; you're the doctor," I replied.

He smiled. "By now, you are the expert on your daughter's autism. I need to consult with an expert."

After my comment on the fee, I sat there and bawled my eyes out. It was the first time I cried.

Maybe it was all the times I thought my daughters' ways were in my imagination, or the look I got from family when I forbid them to wear yellow in my house.

The whispers that I was over exaggerating her meltdowns.

Loud sounds hurt her eyes; loud colors hurt her ears.

Low functioning/high functioning.

No tags, creases, or seams.

She's spoiled, she needs discipline. Finding food she will eat that ISN'T orange.

Eats her food like a dog eats out of a bowl. Silverware is out to hurt her.

It all came out. Complete with mascara running down my face.

It's okay to cry. Fall to your knees bawl your eyes out. Shake your fists to the skies.

When you're finished, get up, brush yourself off, fix your hair.

You are not crazy. Step into the light, no more hiding in darkness, from anyone.

Your child is autistic. It's not a death sentence. It's a way of living.

This was the day I started to write.

What would I call this book and why?

I had a few ideas.

"Diary of a Mad White Autistic Mother."

"The A in autism is for Alien."

"Newspaper Reads."

Finally, it hit me.

"Autism: Rabbit Ears to Cable"

There was a time when cable did not exist. Oh yes, TV had metal sticks on top of them called antennas. Later they were referred to as rabbit ears.

When you had a program coming on, you started arranging the antennas, trying to bring the picture into focus. The screen had snow.

The bodies looked like they were swimming across the screen. Bodies trying to reconnect with their heads.

We would apply tin foil to the rabbit ears to attach wire hangars. We never did have a clear picture.

In the 1980s, cable appeared to the public, if you were lucky enough to afford it. In my case, I dated a cable guy who hooked it up for me illegally. That story is not important right now.

I stood in my living room, anticipating what the picture screen would look like. Soon there it was.

A picture came across the screen. My mouth dropped open. No adjustments needed.

Colors were vibrant, no snow, just smooth clear screen. It was like a halo was over the TV as the angels sang out.

With cable, everything became clear.

When it comes to understanding autism, we all had rabbit ears before we ever had cable.

On my quest to understand autism, I have talked to hundreds of parents of autistics.

I've divided them into five groups.

All believe they have the facts backed up by studies, as to what causes autism.

(Group One)
Autism is caused by direct exposure to cell towers, microwave waves, etc.

(Group Two)
Immunizations cause autism.

(Group Three)
Pesticides, ground pollution, bugs, plants etc.

(Group Four)
Autistics are aliens, mutated, much like Marvel's X-Men.

(Group Five)
There's not a damn thing wrong with them.

Autism is a way of living.

In the early years, I became so overloaded with all these theories. I found myself wanting a cure.

As you can see, a cure is not in a group. This is because what would they be cured to?

You take a pill, wake up the next day, you're not you.

Everything you've known about yourself is gone. How you felt about things are gone. Who are you now?

What if you wanted to go back to who you used to be?

This would surely cause a whole new set of problems and possibly huge mental issues.

The people in these groups agree on one thing. Cure is not the answer.

I've settled on #5 with a hint of #4.

It's not that I think my daughter is an alien from outer space.

I have heard her say, "I've been shipwrecked on Earth being forced to live among unintelligent humans."

Think about that. How do you respond? You look up from your dinner plate. She is staring right through you. I wrote #4 in my mashed potatoes.

My mind drifted to John Carpenter's horror flick, "Children of the Damned."

I don't know why. It just did.

It brought back one of our first visits to the research facility.

My son, Pooh, and I entered a lobby.

I was busy adjusting the numerous bags. These bags are filled with things my daughter must have to leave the house. Could be anything from a piece of string to her water bottle she's had for, get this, ten years.

My son was whispering, "Mom, Mom."

Finally, I tune him in. WHAT? He leans over and whispers, "Mom, look at these kids. They all have the same 'Children of the Damned' haircuts."

I slowly lift my head and begin scanning the children in the room, making sure my eyes make no direct contact with anyone.

Sure, enough he was right. They ALL had bowl haircuts at the same length.

I looked at him. Raised one eyebrow, flared nostril, eyes wide open as I jerked my head back in forth.

In our house, this was my signature look. It said don't say another freaking thing.

While my daughter was in her oxygen chamber, my son and I were alone.

"Mom, this is creepy. Don't you think everyone's haircuts look like the damned children?"

Hate me now. I wanted to bust up in laughter because of the way he said it.

I wanted to be respectful. I let out a loud gasp-laugh, immediately followed by my hand quickly covering my mouth.

I'm a horrible person, I'm screaming in my head. I can still hear my son's voice.

"Come on, Mom, you know this is creepy."

Later, I learned that these children had been coming to the center for a parent support group. Sharing problems, finding solutions.

A lot of autistic children have huge meltdowns when it comes to haircuts or styling.

Seems this style of haircut is quick, with no styling, no fuse, no meltdowns.

My daughter wore this haircut for the next five years, not because she had meltdowns at the salon.

She had long hair. She would suck on a large strand of hairs. Drench her hair with saliva. Hair got stronger. Then use the hair to saw into the corner of her mouth.

This is called stimming. Some autistic snap their fingers, some wave their arms, twirl a ribbon to calm themselves. My daughter liked to saw into her mouth. It had to hurt. Yet she shed not a tear.

Headline Reads:

Teacher turns mother in for abused disabled daughter. Mom arrested.

"Children of the Damned" was whispered and laughed about between my two sons.

Over the years, they would find a lot about Pooh, amusing, behind closed doors.

Every time I would catch them making fun of her quirks, they would say, "Mom, you know it's funny. You just can't laugh because you're Mom."

I'm going to admit at times I would have loved to laugh with them. It just felt so wrong.

One time, we were talking about dating. One son says there's no way. She doesn't use silverware. Could you imagine the guy looking at her with her face in a plate?

My other son replies, "Forget dating. How about driving? She's going to need to take her fingers out of her ears to use the steering wheel."

They both could go on if I didn't stop them.

They would tell me they weren't making fun of Pooh, just the autism.

I realize this makes my boys sound heartless, mean, cold. They are not.

Pooh loved going to Circus Circus Casino.

This casino had a trapeze show. Men and women flying through the air. Every time we took her, we got there two hours early in order to get the exact same seat. She had to be in that seat.

On one visit, we got there early only to find a group of pre-teen boys in her seat.

The stage was off from a huge arcade. Maybe they were just kicking it there. I asked them were they here to see the show?

They were cocky boys, telling me, "We don't know."

I asked them could they please move over; my daughter really likes this spot.

One boy says, "We really like this spot."

Fire came up from toes, rapidly moving up my legs, arms, gaining steam on its way up, to blow out my brain.

Who raised these kids?

My boys have been on the receiving end of this fast-moving fire. My oldest son tells me, "I got this, Mom. You don't need to be going to jail."

I didn't see him talk the boys. He must have. The boys moved along to the arcade. Apparently, they now had money to play games. Between both my boys, they came up with 45 dollars to give them to move.

Living in an autistic world is hard on the whole family. Her brothers are very protective of her, love her. They just happen to make fun of autism when she's not around.

As years went by, I decided that if I weren't laughing, I would be crying.

Accept there's no cure for autism.

Autism never sleeps; neither do the parents.

Embrace the shadow, people. Accept your home being more secure than Fort Knox.

You will pack the same lunch, make the same breakfast and dinner 365 days of the year.

Autistics are like socialites. They know a knock-off handbag.

Don't sneak another brand of food, thinking they won't notice. You would be so wrong.

My daughter loved Oscar Mayer beef hot dogs. It was one of the foods she didn't fight because of texture or smell.

I'm in the grocery store, getting the exact same things my daughter has eaten for years, racing through the isles like I'm in the Indy 500.

Don't want to leave the kids out in the car too long.

The boys start arguing, which would set Pooh off for sure.

What's this? I gasped. Oscar Mayer hot dogs are now 100 percent beef.

I grabbed the package, whispering, "No, no, no, it can't be. Why did they do this? Don't they know she's going to notice? How dare they change. That's okay she won't notice, package is the same, they look the same, it's all going to be alright."

I went home, cooked the hotdogs, served them up. She didn't put the hot dog in her mouth. Immediately, she said, "These are not my hot dogs."

"What? Why do you say that? These are Oscar Mayer beef hot dogs."

She points out these hot dogs are darker.

She was right. The 100 percent beef made the color a little darker.

I pleaded with her to try the hot dogs.

She would have nothing to do with the hot dog.

The look on her face. "How dare you try to pass off your Fake Hot Dogs."

I knew that her alien abilities would detect an intruder.

You need to pick and choose your battle with Aussies.

I was going to lose this one. Macaroni and cheese it was.

So many things to learn, deciding what was worth the battle and what will be.

Her fixation with the number seven.

She said goodnight seven times. Hello seven times.

Seven towels.

Seven blankets.

Seven sensory buddies on her bed.

Seven jars of peanut butter.

Seven clocks.

I would try to teach her the numbers one and two were just as good.

She had nothing to do with it.

All day she would walk around the house mumbling six is not seven.

Seven is seven.

Five is not seven…

Seven is seven.

Four is not seven.

Seven is seven.

She would mumble this until she had seven of whatever was missing. It could be days, even weeks.

During the time change, I forgot to set her seven clocks accordingly. Clocks were set the same.

Her iPad had a different time than her clocks.

She must have asked me one hundred times through the night, "What time is it?"

It could drive you totally insane if you couldn't block it out.

Just keep seven of what she likes, problem solved.

One day visiting the research center, I met a mother of an autistic whose child's number was 99. I never complained again.

We discovered that the color bright yellow triggered my daughters stress level.

It was like the color was attacking her. Hiding under tables. Trying to fight her clothes off.

This explains her stress driving at night. I never noticed all the yellow signs along the roads.

Now we throw a blanket over her, and the drive goes on peacefully.

Red was her detour color. I changed all our outlet covers to red. Red placemat in front of the microwave, red kitchen towels hanging off the oven bar.

These were all things she was attracted to. Like a magnet to metal. Stuff that could really hurt her.

Anywhere there was red, she avoided.

Her brothers used this newfound information to their benefit.

They were playing games or other activities; red became the way to keep her away.

Quiet and effective. No more Mom yelling at them to let her sister play with them.

This was very sneaky on their part. But very effective in getting the little sister from pestering them.

Everything about our home became Autism Friendly. Colors. Christmas bells tied to doors alerted us if she were attempting to go wandering around. This wandering is the reason I slept in the living room for years.

I felt I was guarding her if I were upfront, rather in the back of the house in the bedroom.

She is very sensitive to noise, any noise.

To this day, she wears headphones, the same headphones same color, same style.

Years ago, I bought a case of these headphones. I did this to ensure she had the same. I wanted the headphones for the rest of her life.

There wasn't going to be another hot dog incident on my watch.

The bathroom was always an issue. I never noticed how loud a bathroom is until I saw/heard it from her eyes/ears.

Bathtub, shower curtains, flushing toilet, echo, and the dreaded fan.

The bathroom was a battlefield. Everything in it was the enemy of my daughter. As if she were being attacked by a thousand bees.

This included toilet paper, brushing teeth, and when that time came, women menstruation products.

Lord gives me strength. Her body might be ready; she is not. I'm not sure I will survive it myself.

I never stop walking on pins and needles. There was always something my daughter would do that could possibly be mistaken as a felony.

I opened a pet grooming studio. After two years, the shop expanded with pet retail and Doogie Bakery.

In the back of the shop. I created as autistic oasis for my daughter, aka video games.

Between the front of the shop and the back, I kept dog crates ranging from extra small to large.

She could be a handful at the shop.

She used to crawl into the littlest dog crate and go to sleep. I didn't put her in there. She would insist to go in the crate. What the hell? I wasn't going to stop her. She was so crushed in the little crate. She would relax and sleep or lay there and hum.

It made me a nervous wreck; someone would come in the shop and see her in this doggie crate.

The newspaper headline would read, "Disabled girl kept in doggie crate. Mother arrested."

I got pulled over by the police. I must admit I was not speeding. My old car would shake if you went over 35. My car was not shaking.

The officer approached my window.

"Can I see your license and registration?"

As I handed the items over, I asked, "What's this about?"

"I pulled you over because your child was hanging out the window, dropping clothing for at least a half mile."

"WHAT?" I turned around; she appeared to be sleeping under her covers. I see the seatbelt strap leading to her.

I replied, "She's in her seatbelt asleep. That's not possible."

"Lady, you couldn't see her in your mirror."

I was stunned. "No, I did not. I think I would have noticed if she were hanging out the window."

As he was talking to me, another police car pulls up.

Officer had a bundle of what appeared to be clothing in her hands. I recognized the shirt. It was the shirt I had put on her, before we left.

I quickly turned around, reached back, pulled the covers down. There she was nude.

Newspaper reads: "Disabled girl found nude in car. Mother arrested."

If you have an autistic child you will understand, they are invisible, quick, and master escape artists.

If you're going to stay ahead of your Aussie, it's not about what you hear. It's about what you don't hear.

I did not get a ticket.

The officer suggested I keep a better eye on her.

Really? I thought; if I keep a better eye on her, I would need to glue my damn eyeball to her face!

I thanked the officer, grabbed her clothing, and drove off.

I didn't have those childproof gadgets in my car. Are you kidding?

At the time I drove a car, you hit the dashboard to turn on the radio.

My sons referred to the car as the hooptie mobile.

I attached bells on the strap of her seat belt. Jammed a popsicle stick in the outside window, keeping window from being rolled down.

I learned from what could have been a disaster.

I learned about Autism Poof.

Poof they're gone and nobody sees a thing.

Next time, I would need to be even smarter.

This was not the only encounter we would have with my daughter and clothing.

Picture 100 degrees outside.

My daughter wants to go to a wildlife lion preserve.

At this age, she's beginning to wear layers of tight clothing.

She won't go outside without leggings, thick turtleneck, tight winter jacket, hat over pink headphones, knee high boots (she wears to this day).

Living on the ocean, this didn't really present itself a problem.

The average temperature is 65 degrees year-round. You drive 15-20 miles inland.

Temperatures change drastically.

She insisted she did not want to change.

We get to the park. I'm worried she's going to bake alive in her clothes.

I figured once she started walking, she would change her mind. She did not.

The sun was beating down on everyone at the park.

People were fanning themselves in their shorts and summer shirts.

My son brought to my attention that people were staring at us.

"Mom, they're giving you mean looks. Do something or tell them she's autistic. Mom, I heard a woman telling some man, 'Look at that poor little girl, she has to be burning up in those clothes.'"

Why do I need to inform everyone she's autistic? She's not screaming, "I'm hot." Heck, she's not even sweating.

I always sounded so confident and strong on the outside.

Inside, I was on eggshells thinking people thought I was some evil mother.

Along the walk I would nag my daughter to at least take her jacket off.

The more people stared and whispered the more I would insist.

Looking back, insisting she take off her coat was more for all of those staring at us, than being worried about my daughter.

I knew she wasn't going to take her winter clothing off.

I did have short set in the car, just in case someone called the authorities on me.

This wasn't my first rodeo in this situation.

My hair sticking to my forehead, a finger streak through my blush and my heat stress strength deodorant. It claims it won't let you down under stress.

Let me down.

It amazes me that people think I would purposely dress my daughter for snow when it's 100 degrees outside.

I must be an idiot of a mother that should never have children.

You would think, people would assume something must be up with this child, she wasn't whining or crying.

Happy enjoying the lions.

The newspaper reads: "Disabled child exposed to extreme heat denied water. Mother arrested."

My daughter is an adult now. She still layers in winter clothing. Snow boots. She has added a sherpa to her ensemble.

Eating was always a battle.

I would go to sleep at night wondering how she stays healthy on her foods of choice.

Here's that Alien mentality.

All her blood tests and labs would be normal.

I didn't understand it then and I will never understand it.

Autism is a mystery in so many ways.

We surely couldn't force her to use silverware. Maybe we should start with using her fingers.

Anything would be better than putting her face in the plate to eat.

I discovered Pyrex pie plates helped with this training. The curved-up sides. Allowed her to move the food up and out.

This was a huge event in our home.

Eating with her fingers was a battle well-fought.

Visiting thrift stores over the years on the search for pie plates.

We no longer have kitchen plates.

We still use pie plates. Wherever we go, we carry a pie plate.

I've gotten used to people staring at our table as I transfer food from restaurant plates to her Pyrex Pie plate.

A lot of meltdowns have happened in restaurants.

Maybe it was the radio, people talking, plates clacking.

It all would run her under the table, rolling herself into a ball with her fingers in her ear. We left her there.

The alternative is screaming while all these noises attack her. It could be heard down the street.

Our little town had a radio station.

Every morning, the lady DJ would have a "What would you do?" scenario.

They would open the phone lines to callers.

This morning, I'm driving the kids to school, like usual, running on caffeine and little sleep.

We had been to a restaurant the night before.

It wasn't the quietest visit.

My mother had joined us. Making her case, if I applied discipline to my daughter, she would have to use silverware.

As my boys used to say, "Sometimes you've just got to release Pooh on people."

I told my mom, "Go ahead, Mother. You try." (One eyebrow up.)

My mother jumped on the chance to show me that my daughter had a discipline problem more than an Autistic problem.

After 20 minutes my daughter was in meltdown mode.

Mother's nerves were shot.

She went outside.

Must have taken her 10 cigarettes to calm herself.

The repercussions of my mother's attempt were felt through the night.

My hair stood on end with wild, sleepy eyes.

The question of the morning is: what would you do if a child is causing a scene in a restaurant?

What? Were they at the restaurant last night?

The lady DJ says: "if I saw a child acting out, I would go up to the table. Suggest they take the child outside to calm down."

I flung the car off the road. Parked. Dialed the radio station.

They put me through.

The lady DJ asks, "Hello, what's your comment?"

Boy, did I have a comment.

"Big of you to think, you know what's going on at that table. Maybe the parents are holding their ground with the child. Possibly the child has a disability of some kind. If you walked up to my table suggesting I take my child outside to calm down, I would tell you to take yourself outside and calm down!"

Now I don't know why people heard me say: she and I step outside.

As if I'm challenging her to a fight.

This morning radio call was the topic of the day.

All over our small little town.

Newspaper Reads: "Caller threatens DJ with physical violence. Women arrested."

Living in an autism world is a lot of sheer panic.

For you and the others that just don't understand

My mother used to say you wouldn't believe it unless you lived it. Referring to the autism world.

One of the things my daughter would eat wasn't orange was Eggos.

Kellogg's homestyle Eggos.

No substitutes.

She ate two Eggos, at the same time, every day, for over 22 years.

I'm no mathematician. However, that's approximately 16,000 Eggos.

Let that sink in.

FALL 2009

Atlanta Georgia

Factory where Eggos are made shut down.

Major flooding produced bacteria.

No time estimated on how long it would be before the factory was up and running.

There would be an Eggo shortage.

THIS CANNOT HAPPEN.

I went to the two major supermarkets in town. I bought all the Eggos they said they had. I'm still not sure they were telling the truth.

I believe it was six boxes. Each contained eight Eggos.

I went to a supercenter; they had none.

This wasn't going to be enough.

I'm frantic. This cannot be happening.

There was a small neighborhood market down by us.

I explained I had to get my hands on more Eggos. The Eggo factory was shut down.

I know it sounds crazy.

If my daughter doesn't have her Eggos, the world is truly going to end in our house. Aka no one sleeps.

They knew me and my family.

They told me Eggos come in cases.

Stores break up the case to sell individually.

They contacted their food distributors to check their warehouses.

Apparently, these warehouses hold bulk of foods.

Bingo, they had Eggos.

I pleaded with them to order all the cases.

When they arrived, it was 50 cases of Homestyle Eggos with 24 Eggos in each individual box.

How in the hell am I going to pay for this?

Where in the hell am I going to put them?

I was so stressed out over not finding any.

I wasn't thinking on cost and storage.

As with many things with autism and finances.

We held a car wash.

Bought used freezers and Eggos.

You couldn't get through our house without running into freezers full of waffles.

Headline Read: "Women threatening violence at stores for Eggos. Women arrested."

As we pass into teen Autism, things get more challenging.

Just because she's autistic doesn't mean, at times, there isn't a teenage girl inside my daughter.

One evening, we are watching Avengers.

IT HAPPENS.

She just blurts out when she sees Iron Man, her stomach feels fuzzy.

WHAT? HUH?

Did my Pooh just say a boy is cute?

I have been waiting for this mother-daughter moment. BOY TALK.

Get the popcorn, strike up the band. I jumped from my chair. Crossed my legs on the floor next to her.

Took a huge breath to calm myself down.

Soooo what is it you find cute about Iron Man?

She looked at me like I tried to give her a green vegetable, and proceeded to tell me all about the hidden powers of Euro cat and the 59 stages on which he has evolved.

This girl inside my daughter was there for a moment. Poof, she was gone.

As my daughter gets older, this girl makes more appearances. In fact, a lot of questions on sexuality.

Autistics can be very highly sensory sensitive.

Why it surprises parents that their adult aussies will apply those same things sexually. Should be no surprise.

We all know it.

Yet parents are afraid to talk about masturbation/exploration.

I suggest you address it.

Many adult autistics are highly sexual.

You don't want them to be fathers and mothers when they literally can't take care of themselves or a baby.

With the help from doctors, I decided that birth control shot would stop menstruation and protect her.

These are tough decisions.

Each parent will need to make the decision best for them.

We did try a few menstrual cycles.

It terrified her. She harmed herself during her period.

This led to our decision. Well, that and I met too many parents raising their autistics children who got pregnant while at school. With another autistic.

Autistics are very smart. My daughter can tell you how many moons orbit Saturn.

She can't tie her shoes or tell you what she had for lunch.

She has the same thing every day.

My daughter can tell you how a cliff is made. The dangers of standing near a cliff, as she walks off the cliff.

My mother was visiting.

She liked to keep her curling iron on in the bathroom.

I have told my mother be careful.

Pooh can lull you into a false sense of security.

Giving you all info you need to feel comfortable about her safety!

When I returned, my mom had an astonished look on her face.

She claimed bay knew the curling iron was hot. It could burn her.

My mom exclaimed POOF bay disappeared.

She ran to the bathroom, and found Pooh holding the curling iron.

It was that incident my mother started coming around.

She would stay with us months at a time.

My mom became famous for telling people, "Unless you've seen Autism with your own eyes, you just can't believe it."

Early years of autism, Pooh spoke in kitten purrs or lion roars.

Now she speaks English and Japanese. Not broken Japanese. Very fluent.

I believe she picked it up from watching anime. Japanese cartoons.

She can go days without speaking.

Other weeks in Japanese.

I know more about anime than I ever wanted to. I had to watch if I were going to communicate with her.

We attend anime conventions. We go dressed in anime costumes.

Who knew there was an anime world in the states?

I hear about anime all year long. Everyday.

There are times I just can't talk about it anymore.

I tell her, "Mom needs a break."

Why it bothers me if anyone else says they need a break after only 15 minutes, I get upset.

If you haven't paid your autism dues in this house, you don't get to escape until you've listened for at least an hour.

This very well could be why we never had company.

Headline reads: "People held captive and tortured in a home. Women arrested."

Mimicking is another charm autistics have.

Everything she has learned for a correct response to a question she does by repeating what she sees and hears on TV.

If you say to her, "Hello, how are you?"

She panics, not knowing the correct response.

Her brain starts filing through hundreds of TV files in her brain, eventually finding appropriate responses.

"Well, hello. I am doing exceptionally well tonight."

Even though it's morning.

It's not a perfect science, but it works for her.

Before my sons grew up and headed into their own life, they discovered something about their sister. It all started with simple child's card game.

Pooh can count cards.

At first, they didn't know what to do with this ability of their sister.

As they grew older and saw some Casino movies, they developed a plan.

It was more of a pact between them.

When Pooh turned 21, they would take her to Vegas.

Pooh will be their road to riches.

I would tell them it's illegal to count cards. People get thrown out of casinos for that. Maybe jail.

"Oh, come on, Mom. Hit each casino a little card playing at each. Get out before they suspect anything?"

"Never," I told them.

"Mom, you can say that now." (Putting his arm around my shoulder) "But you can't live forever."

My dear sons.

Loves of my life.

Even if do leave this earth.

At this point, I'm not sure I am.

I assure you both.

Haunting you will be my mission approved by God himself.

You think I made your life tough alive. (Each arm around both boys) Wait until I'm a ghost.

My sons grew up and headed into their own lives.

I need to admit, I miss them. I miss their help and understanding.

I miss their autism humor.

It's not the same laughing about autism with people that think you are going to hell for laughing at all.

I suppose that will be one of those "Family Secrets."

Life without the boys took adjustment.

They don't say it.

It must feel liberating to be free of the autism insanity.

At the same time, the women they marry must know.

Their life will someday include my daughter.

This scares me the most.

My sons have brought home many girls for me to meet.

These girls tried to make a huge impression on my sons by fawning all over their sister.

As if they think, if my autistic sister likes you, then you're the women for me.

My sons laugh at that too.

They know it's not about if my autistic sister likes you.

It's how long can you sit, while sister explains, in detail, her favorite Pokémons.

All 412 out of the 1,008.

Pooh doesn't like or dislike anyone.

She could care less.

She doesn't lie. She doesn't understand the concept.

She will point out your little white lies in front of anyone.

If I say to someone, "It's nice to see you again."

Pooh will repeat exactly what you said earlier.

"That woman gets on my nerves."

Believe me, my Pooh has led me to spitting out my coffee to choking on my saliva.

This could explain my lack of friends.

Possibly why a guest's first words, upon arriving at my house, are "I can't stay long."

My oldest son, Chris, was born when I was 16.

I was a baby having a baby.

Full of fear, questions.

I took motherhood very importantly.

I traded my childhood for parenthood, leaving my friends, young life, behind. I never married his father.

We did manage to hang onto our relationship for ten years.

Things were challenging as a young mom still in high school.

It took a long time before I could think about another baby.

My youngest son, Dylan, was born ten years later with my husband.

What a torpedo, from the time I gave birth to him until this day.

Five years later, I had Pooh.

Learning as a teen mom was behind me.

I had adjusted my parenting skills with a Torpedo Child.

I had the experience. I was ready for this baby.

Pooh through me for a curve.

This baby cried to be put down, not to be picked up.

This baby could lay in a wet diaper; unless you checked, she didn't bother you.

She didn't want breast milk. Formula it is. (This was good news for me as I did not like breastfeeding)

If you put her next to you in bed, she cried. If you left her in the crib, she didn't cry.

Newborns generally wake you every two hours, crying for a diaper change or to eat.

Not this newborn. If she woke up, you would never know it. She would be awake, just not crying.

I set my alarm for every two hours to wake myself up for feeding.

At her well baby doctor appointments, everything was fine. I was told she was a healthy baby.

I would tell them about how easy she was.

They told me how great that was. It made them jealous.

Followed by a short story about how their babies would be exhausting.

As she got into her toddler stage, she didn't need to be entertained. She would sit and spin her bottle for hours if you let her.

Compared to the boys, this was a perfect, healthy baby.

I'll say it again.

Pooh was a perfect baby!

Insight. Perfect babies cry.

They cry to be fed, cry to be changed, cry to be held.

Up every few hours.

Wants for your attention.

Their crying makes you cry.

I enjoyed this easy baby.

Nothing ever crossed my mind that anything was wrong.

It wasn't until she was two years old.

I started noticing things.

I wrote her oddities off as Pooh just goes to the beat of a different drummer.

My imagination.

Not all kids play Peek-A-Boo covering their ears, despite you covering your eyes?

So what if she only points at things she wants?

I had a doctor tell me she points because she doesn't need to ask.

Discipline her.

When it came to baby foods, she only ate foods that were orange.

I would make the food orange with a little food coloring, in order to balance her diet.

One morning, our oldest son was changing her diaper.

I hear, "MOM, Pooh is orange!"

"WHAT?" I walk to his side.

Her skin was orange.

I rushed her to her pediatrician.

I did not call.

I ran into the office.

Something's wrong with my baby!

Yellow is a sign of jaundice.

WHAT HORRIBLE DISEASE makes an orange baby?

Arriving, I was so loud the doctor could hear me in the back.

The nurse escorted us back into the exam room.

I began to unwrap my baby.

First thing asked, "What's the last thing she ate?"

"WHAT… oh, it was oatmeal."

(Lightbulb over my head)

I explained Pooh throwing a fit if the foods were not orange.

I explained I was concerned about her not eating other foods.

This morning, I added two drops of orange food coloring in her oatmeal.

The box said nontoxic.

"OH, MY LAWRD, did I poison my baby?"

"You didn't poison her," the doctor replied.

"I am wondering about orange."

"Babies generally don't distinguish colors to taste."

"WELL, this one does. SHE KNOWS. If food isn't orange, she becomes highly agitated. You think this is in my head. Stop right there."

"We have put her through tests."

"It's not the taste, it's the color."

"Hummm," he mumbles. "Well, if that's true—"

"IT IS," I interrupted.

Doctor went on to suggest, "Don't use so much food coloring. Use it in water, not with milk. Milk makes it hard for the body to break down the dye. It will come out through the skin and urine."

"It doesn't come out in her urine," I explained.

"Yes, it does," he replied.

"No, I change her diaper. There's no orange."

"Her stool?" he asked.

"Nope."

"Well, isn't she an odd little girl?" The doctor smiled, as he lifted her little finger.

He had no idea had odd she would grow to be.

I never used food coloring again.

A study had come out that Red 40 could cause cancer.

I turned to a more organic method.

I bought cans of tomato sauce, beets, etc.

I would mix colors with these reds until I got the perfect shade of orange.

I felt like a mad scientist.

Mixing potions, by a faint light, on top of a crumbling desk, in a basement deep within a castle.

As she got older, if you put orange slices on her pie plate, she would start to eat some foods that wasn't orange.

Later, it turned to sniffing and touching her food before eating.

Not sure what she was sniffing or feeling for.

She knew. That's all that mattered.

Pooh did like popcorn.

She had to have it at 12 p.m.

Not 11:59 or 12:05.

At 12 p.m.

Things like this made the thought of school terrifying.

School was coming.

Didn't matter how I felt.

I was no teacher.

I would surely go to jail for not enrolling her.

Boy, secretly I gave it some thought.

My daughter would soon enter a world that was not her own. Surely not designed for her.

School years brought most of my aging process, way before it was time.

Public school was where I heard the word Autistic for the first time.

I've been a teacher for twenty years. Hundreds of students. Your daughter needs to be tested for autism.

The lower grades in elementary school were the easiest.

Children had forgiving and patient natures.

The higher elementary grades, kids changed.

I know it wasn't my daughter. She was the same.

My aussie had no grasp on playground etiquette.

It doesn't take long before children understand the ways of the playground.

The line for the swing.

Pooh would just cut in line.

With her lack of expression, when she cut in, she appeared almost arrogant, when she really is oblivious to the rules.

You can't see autism.

Until she speaks.

She's just another normal child.

Perhaps this contributed to her being picked on by other children.

Remember, her number is seven.

There was always a line at the water fountain.

She took her time to sip water, swallow, breathe. Repeat seven times.

Kids would begin their pushing at the end of the line.

Working the push up until it reached Pooh.

The push never phased her.

One day, I was called to the school.

She was at the water fountain.

A kid had pushed her head into the fountain, claiming she was holding up the line on purpose.

Pooh would come home.

I would find little pieces of pencil lead in the hat on her jacket.

I asked her about it.

"It was raining pencils," she answered.

I knew kids were flicking pieces of pencil lead at her.

If she growled or hissed, well, that just initiated other acts of cruelty.

I heard many times, "If she would just... If she just wouldn't... If she would just stop this or that."

All said by teachers.

Her brothers would try and teach her to talk differently and act differently.

I would scold them about pushing her to be different.

The boys would tell me, "She's going to get beat up, Mom."

Their efforts weeded no results.

"Mom, buy her a shirt that says, 'I'm autistic.'"

At least people would know there's something wrong with her.

My boys asked me to do this many times over the years.

My daughter never did make friends with anyone.

First day of school, you could see the cliques forming with the girls.

I dressed Pooh top of the fashion, looking very stylish.

Boots to match every outfit.

I did this to help her fit in.

The first day of school, girls gathered around her.

Next day, not one girl would come near her.

I pulled her out of public school in the fifth grade.

After, the teacher had left the room to walk Pooh to the restroom.

Before she got back, kids hid her headphones. Moved her things.

Changed out her favorite chair.

When Pooh returned, she melted down.

Crawling under the desk with her fingers in her ears.

I enrolled her in a charter school.

You could attend or homeschool.

Pooh attended.

Day before she started school.

The charter administration addressed the class about autism.

Such a relief.

I would go to bed worried about Pooh going to school every weekday.

On the weekends, I went to sleep fearing Monday coming.

It all starts again.

I would fall asleep biting my lip and grinding my teeth.

I would wake up.

My jaw felt wired shut.

My mouth frozen in the tight lip position.

Half of the next day, I walked around with no lips, clenched jaw.

My mother would say, "Sum, don't hold your jaw and lips like that. It very unattractive."

"Yes, Mother."

I wouldn't be so hideous after lunch.

My daughter was free to be herself, stuff cat stitches (ten-year-old stitched up stuffed cat) in one hand and IEP in the other.

A long cat tail attached to the back of her leggings. Not a single thing was ever said by the kids.

I was like the MIB (Men in Black).

Only I am MIB (Moms in Black).

If something were going on, I would know.

My sons could testify to my skills and knowledge.

MIB caused them many issues, which led them to doing time (restriction).

Two more items about school.

IEP

(Individualized Education Plan)

This plan is put together by all your teachers, principals, special education teachers, occupational therapists, and you.

All in one meeting.

This plan involves studying accommodations, testing accommodations, in class accommodations. This could be anything from longer test time too not sitting by a class Bell.

Whatever your child needs to be successful is in this report.

Everyone at the meeting must sign the agreement.

The key.

Everyone involved in your child's IEP should be at the meeting and sign.

If they are not, you will never know if they are aware of the accommodations made for your child.

IEP meetings are once a year, unless another one is requested.

Meetings are held after school, lasting about hour half.

If one staff member does not show up, I would reschedule.

Your child is that important.

This is the one shot to cover all your child's needs.

The longest IEP meeting ever recorded at this school was four hours, by yours truly.

Practice those pencil pushups. Work on that one eyebrow up. Tune up seat shifting and those power leg crossings.

It's a Damn IEP meeting.

Power is with the parent.

Over the years, I would question teachers, if something were in Pooh's IEP and it wasn't being applied in the classroom.

"I'm sure it's not in IEP," teacher would say.

"Well, maybe it's time for another IEP meeting?"

The response was always, "Oh, I don't think that's necessary," said with panic-stricken eyes.

I need to thank the honest teachers. I LOVE you all.

I knew she was in good hands with you.

You come driving up. Pick up your child.

Teacher opens the door.

"How was she today?" I asked.

"OH, SHE'S SUCH A JOY, very nice to have my class." BIG smile.

My eyes would stare at her like deer in headlights.

Give me this teacher any day.

"How was she today?"

"We got through it together. I do believe it will be a three-glass wine night though," smiles the teacher.

YES, that is my daughter. Hard, complicated, exasperating, challenging, make your hair stand on end, worthy Autistic child.

Telling me any differently makes you and everything you say just noise.

I don't want Autism to overshadow my boys' struggles.

My commitment to them was just as strong.

My oldest, Chris, started martial arts when he was four years old, earning degrees in many Black Belts.

A lot of competitions with weekly dojo training.

He did struggle in school.

Arguments with him about his grades were endless.

High school senior year was no different.

I received notices he was in danger of not graduating weekly.

In one of our most memorable discussions, he walked toward his cave (his bedroom), leaving me at the head of the hallway.

He stopped, turned to me, and said, "Mom, I'm not as smart as you think I am."

Chris stared straight at me, as if he were looking for me to have that AHA moment.

"You're not as stupid as you think you are either."

I slam back at him, like a tennis ball being slammed over the net.

It was me that delivered his AHA moment.

He did graduate.

My youngest son, Dylan, his father was walking him across a crosswalk against the light.

A car slammed into my four-year-old son, hitting him twice before landing in the gutter.

He suffering Traumatic Brain Injury and was in a coma for nine days.

I was told he would never walk or talk again.

He walked, talked, and drove up to his graduation.

My daughter, despite all her educational, social, and personal challenges, many school days missed due to heavy rain drops, research studies, doctor appointments located eight hours one way from our home, graduated.

Everyone is growing up now.

Finding out who they are.

My oldest went into the Navy, spending years on a Submarine.

My son, Dylan, had won scholarships in agriculture.

He began working for the rest of tuition on a local dairy farm.

I mentioned earlier in the book, watching specials with Autistics doing incredible things, singing, playing sports and driving, TV shows depicting Autistics as doctors, lawyers, investigators, always brings up the question: when does pushing your teen autistic turn to mistreating them?

Driving a motor vehicle.

She never expressed interest.

I felt a need for her to decide by experiencing it.

Pooh memorized the DMV handbook, front to back.

She could tell you exactly what page to find vehicle codes, vehicle violations, car upkeep.

She couldn't drive a car.

I pushed, encouraged, put her in the driver's seat, hired a driving school.

He said there was no way she should ever drive.

He couldn't believe I enrolled her in driving school.

I got a second opinion.

I was told she would be a danger to others on the road.

The instructor refused to put her life on the line trying to teach her.

I cannot teach her. In attempts in empty parking lots, my gums started bleeding.

My lips sustained permanent scarring from me biting to keep from passing out from fear!

In my heart, I knew she couldn't. What if I were wrong?

Or what if I were not trying hard enough?

How far is too far, before pushing turns into cruelty?

For both parent and autistic.

I made the decision not to battle driving.

In attempts to have her shop for groceries, within ten minutes, she was spinning around in circles, covering her eyes, mumbling.

"My eyes are on fire. Call 911."

How many times do you subject her to this?

The answer came during Covid.

Home delivery.

On the site, I create a shopping list.

She goes to the site and clicks on what she needs.

Employment

There are regional centers that help employ adults with certain handicaps.

Seems they had great success.

We tried Pooh at different jobs. Jobs around her abilities and needs.

I stopped dropping her off and going home.

Instead, I would park, waiting for that phone call to come get her.

With Pooh, some days, she's eight months old, complete with pacifier; other days, she's up to 88 years old, attached with a list of her aches and pains.

Some days, she speaks like a professor, astrologist, philosopher.

Other days in Japanese, purrs, or not speaking at all.

At this writing, we are still working on maybe someday, she can hold a job.

My daughter does not remember much of her childhood.

When I ask her about her memories, she draws a blank.

I think about all the memories that entails.

I cannot wrap my mind around it.

I show her pictures.

She has no memory.

If she does recall something, she has no details.

I can't forget.

Remembering everything I do could explain my need to be on anti-depressants and a good hair color with extra gray coverage.

Adult Autism

A book that's still being written.

More to learn.

In her younger days, she was never comfortable with her body.

In her teens as breasts started coming in, she wanted them off.

She didn't mind the hair under her arms or on her legs.

Deodorant and acne medicine felt horrible on her skin.

Her being a girl, I pushed these things.

I asked the therapist to help.

"Who is the acne really bothering?" she asked.

"I guess me," I replied.

"Do you want me to work on battles that bother you?"

"If that's the case, she doesn't care her armpits smell like onions or if her breath is bad. Her whole hygiene is no problem for her. Does that mean we should let her walk around like that?"

Her answer to me was, "Being we have very few battles to win, what do you think is most important?"

My reply did not include her acne.

Showering, teeth, deodorant took center stage.

I can't say I wasn't disappointed.

I wanted her to be girly. Shaving, eyebrows, styling her hair, nails, smelling pretty.

The doctor was right. These things are important to me.

As an adult, she prefers not to identify with any gender.

If she thinks about gender, it would mean acknowledging body parts. She prefers to ignore "Their Existence."

Another development in her adulthood.

By this point, there wasn't any more room for more things keeping me up at night.

This new thing crept as I drove.

I would be driving and the thought of accepting this as a real thing, a reality would make me shiver.

Almost like trying to shake it off.

Drive, shiver, and repeat.

Why was I shiver driving?

Schediaphilia

sche-dia-phi-li-a.

A person's attracted to animated characters.

The attraction can lead to love, emotional attachment, or sexual arousal.

Animatesexual

Anime-Sexual.

People who have difficulty being attracted to real people.

They have not ruled out real people all together.

They also find themselves drawn to Japanese anime characters.

My mother had not visited in a few months.

She too wondered if Pooh would ever be interested in boys.

She arrived.

Pooh just blurted out she had a boyfriend.

"WHAT? Huh?" I stuttered.

"Well, Pooh, tell me all about him."

My mother smiled and gave me that look like, "She's cured."

"His name is Waldo. He has blue hair," Pooh struggled to say.

Well, now Ninny (my mom) wanted to hear everything about him.

Pooh turned her iPad on and turns the screen to my mom.

Her eyes got big, nodding her head. "Oh, I see."

"He's very handsome."

On the screen was a character on an anime show with an anime boy named Waldo.

This was my 14-year-old daughter's first boyfriend. She loved him very much.

He was a part of her life for years.

She broke it off with him at 16, moving on to other possibilities.

I've come to understand Pooh's schediaphilia and animesexual.0

These relationships went into her 20s.

Pooh remains closed off about gender.

She did announce she was bisexual.

Where this goes, new thing goes. I keep my fingernails down to nubs.

Like many things about my daughter and autism, things remain a mystery.

My daughter was not popular with the kids or the teachers.

It really makes you question humanity.

It seems human nature tells you if the disability is invisible, then it doesn't exist.

I wanted to throw Pooh a birthday.

I knew the kids in her class would not come if Bailee handed them invitations.

Little creepers.

I went around them. I knew most of the parents.

I handed them invitations. Made the time around dinner hour at a pizza Parlor.

Nearly everyone showed up.

Pooh sat a bench rearranging her Pokemon cards, like she had done hundreds of times.

Three kids stopped off at her table, never staying long.

The party was okay.

Then it was over.

Pooh went on and on about three of her Gold Pokemon cards that were missing.

Her brother, in the navy, had stopped off in Japan.

This is the origin of Pokemon.

He found her four rare gold cards.

We searched and searched, but never did find them.

Pooh went on about these cards 24/7 for approximately two months.

Six months later, the local newspaper wanted to do an article on autism.

April is Autism Awareness Month.

They wanted to feature my daughter.

The article took up two pages.

If you didn't know my daughter was autistic, you would now.

Two weeks after the article, Pooh received a letter in the mail.
I opened it up.
Two Golden Pokemon cards fell out.
Her missing cards.
The letter read:

Dear Pooh,
I saw you in the newspaper.
I didn't know you had autism.
Every day, I have been very mean to you.
I did things I should not.
I let others be mean to you.
I don't know if you can forgive me.
I want to start over and be your friend forever.
When I was at your birthday, I stole two of your Pokemon cards.
I kept them safe. I knew they were special cards.
I am returning them to you.
I should not have done that.
I asked God to forgive me.
You didn't deserve meanies.
I don't blame you for never wanting to be my friend.
I'm giving you my phone number and address.
I hope you call someday.

My daughter grabbed the cards, scampered to her room.
Never asking a single question about the letter.
Myself, I reread the letter, later in the night.
Suspecting your child is being bullied is one thing.
Knowing it was happening every day, dropping her off into a war zone, my heart broke. I cried myself to sleep.
I woke up with a new addition to tight lips, clenched jaw.
Non-waterproof mascara. I added racoon eyes.
My son gasped. "Mom, you can't drive me to school like that. You look like a Tweeker."
HEADLINE READS: "Mother arrested transporting child under the influence of drugs."

Divorce and Autism is a story that needs to be written.

A recent study shows 85 percent of marriages, with autistic children, end in divorce.

I am not going to say my daughter caused my divorce.

Autism brought stresses.

My daughter did not.

I decided our daughter would live at home.

My husband's choice was an assisted living facility.

When two people see their future differently, it is a huge problem.

So is infidelity.

After 17 years, we divorced.

Home to homeless.

Food stores to food banks.

Money in the bank to zero balance.

Business owner to business closed.

All while trying to raise autism.

It took seven years to rebuild my life without bringing a man into the mix.

After ten years I was ready to test the dating waters.

The book.

Living Single with autism by your side.

A guide to dating, and if you're lucky, a relationship.

It is a book also waiting to be written.

My boys never argued on who will take care of Pooh when I die.

Seems they're more concerned about where I'll be spending my ailing years.

"You're taking her. No, you're taking her."

"HELLO, I'm sitting right here and can hear you both."

Headline Reads: "Boys hit in head with frying pan. Mother arrested."

Autism is filled With Headline Reads:

Most of what you read is not what it appears to be.

I've met thousands of moms of autistics.

All live on the edge.

I can't tell you how many times I looked at Pooh's adult pacifier and thought, I wonder if it would help.

It would be just my luck.

I would get caught sucking on the thing.

A lot of people use them in sexual role play. Adult stores carry them.

Many autistics, like my Pooh, use them when they age regress.

NEWSPAPER READS: "Kids subjected to sex toys. Mother arrested."

Parenting autistics is a lonely life.

Letting people in your circle is not easy.

I applaud you all for doing something that's meant to mentally take you down.

I said in the beginning of the book, my life, with autism, needs acceptance and laughter, or I will find myself in a corner, rocking, sucking my thumb, asking has anyone seen my baseball?

I do have a baseball in a ball case, on a shelf in my bedroom.

I did not purchase it.

The inscription reads, "I want to be the one who helps you find your baseball. Love, Michael."

I dedicate this book to Pooh.

Without you, I would have seen the world with rabbit ears.

Cable showed me a whole new world with such clarity, love, understanding, and patience.

Thank you.

My love.

My daughter.